GRADES = MONEY
A Proven System to Rapidly Improve High School Grades

Guy M. Kezirian, MD, FACS

For more information, updates, and useful learning tools, visit
www.GradesEqualMoney.com

Copyright 2013 © Guy M. Kezirian
All Rights Reserved

First Printing: April 2013
10 9 8 7 6 5 4 3 2 1

ISBN: 1490562958
ISBN 13: 9781490562957
Library of Congress Control Number: 2012923692

*Dedicated to Robert M. Rochefort,
an inspirational teacher and true friend.*

TABLE OF CONTENTS

Introduction III

PART 1: THE WHY AND HOW OF ACTIVE LEARNING

    Chapter 1: Grades = Money 3

    Chapter 2: Are you ready? Take this quiz. 11

    Chapter 3: The Five Techniques of Active Learning . . 21

PART 2: CREATE AN ACTIVE LEARNING CULTURE

    Chapter 4: Take Control 39

    Chapter 5: The Importance of Friends 51

    Chapter 6: Teachers 59

PART 3: ADVANCED ACTIVE LEARNING TECHNIQUES

    Chapter 7: Active Listening 69

    Chapter 8: Active Reading 81

    Chapter 9: Active Studying 93

PART 4: MAKING IT HAPPEN

    Chapter 10: Be an Active Student 105

    An Afterword to Educators 115

    Acknowledgments 119

    About the Author 121

> *"You have to expect things of yourself before you can do them."*
> —Michael Jordan

INTRODUCTION

Money is important.

Money may not buy happiness but it does buy food, clothes, cars, and the many other necessities and comforts of life. Anyone who says money is not important is probably not paying the bills.

Because money is important, grades are important. Good grades will make it possible to earn good money. Your grades may not make you money today, during high school, but they will later on. Good grades result in college admission, scholarships, job offers, and other opportunities.

What kind of lifestyle will your grades purchase? Will they make it possible to buy nice cars, clothes, and good food? Will they support your hopes and dreams?

Not everyone can be a straight-A student, but most students are far more intelligent than their grades would indicate. Do your grades reflect your potential? If not, do you know why?

Grades measure *academic performance*, not intelligence. Grades are based on exam scores and whether the schoolwork matched the teacher's expectations. They are not based on a student's potential, desire, or intelligence.

In turn, the ability to perform academically relies on *skill*. Skills are based on techniques, which can be learned. Students who earn good grades are not necessarily smarter. They just have good learning skills.

This book will teach you the skills and techniques you need to earn good grades.

Even though grades do not measure intelligence, students are often labeled as "smart," "not so smart," or even "slow" based on their grades. These labels can have lasting and often damaging effects that can limit opportunities both during high school and after graduation.

The labels often become a self-fulfilling prophesy, too. Poor grades lead to low morale, which leads to disinterest and

Introduction

then to worse grades. On the other hand, good grades often inspire confidence and better achievement. Figure 1 illustrates how grades impact a student's self-image and affect future performance. This cycle is all too familiar to underperforming students.

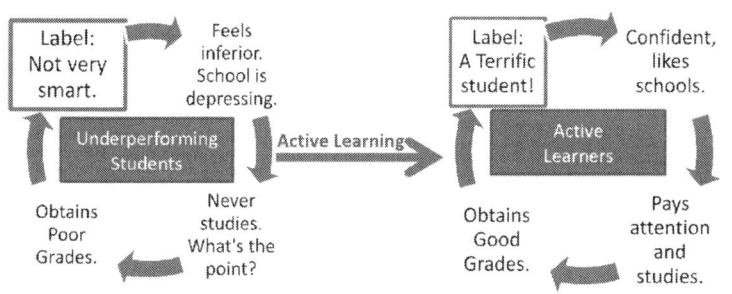

Figure 1: The cycle between grades, academic achievement and teacher feedback becomes a self-fulfilling prophecy in both positive and negative ways. Active Learning skills can make the difference.

The purpose of this book is to break the cycle of academic underperformance and move students to the right side of the diagram to bring grades in line with ability. The skills needed to perform well at school are developed through a process called "Active Learning."

Active Learning gives students control over the learning process. It not only makes it possible to earn good grades; it develops skills that are useful throughout life.

The most difficult part of becoming an active learner is acknowledging the need to do so. This takes maturity, resolve, and confidence. So, congratulations! You have completed the hardest step and have overcome the emotional resistance to change. The rest of the process is straightforward.

I wish you every success.

Guy M. Kezirian, MD, FACS

PART I

THE WHY AND HOW OF ACTIVE LEARNING

> *"Education is an ornament in prosperity and a refuge in adversity."*
> —Aristotle

CHAPTER 1
GRADES = MONEY

Education is like a ladder. How high we climb determines our level in society and directly impacts how much money we will earn. It takes good grades to move up the ladder. Depending on the level, moving up might mean advancing to the next grade, being accepted into a university, winning a scholarship, or landing a job. Good grades are what make it possible to climb higher. Grades unlock doors and create opportunities.

The picture on the next page illustrates this concept with real numbers. Notice how income increases with each level of education. Society puts a dollar value on school achievement. On average, the higher you go, the more you earn.

> ### Skill Development Tips
>
> *This book is written for students. Parents, teachers, and friends can support students by reading it, too, but Active Learning requires students to engage.*
>
> *Skill Development Tips and Chapter Summaries are provided throughout this book to guide students on how to proceed. Readers can use these tips to ease into the program and avoid feeling overwhelmed by excessive detail.*

Trying to compete in the workplace without a degree is difficult. If two people apply for a high-level job and one has a degree and the other does not, the one with the degree is usually going to win.

Of course, not everyone is suited for college. What about jobs that do not require a college education? In that case, technical training may be needed. The ladder metaphor applies equally well to those pursuits. Higher training brings more income.

WHY BOTHER?

Money is important, and it becomes more important over time. This is especially true when there isn't enough money!

The fact that you are reading this book suggests that you understand—perhaps in the back of your mind—that doing well in school matters to your future. Good grades make it possible to advance through the educational system. Grades bring

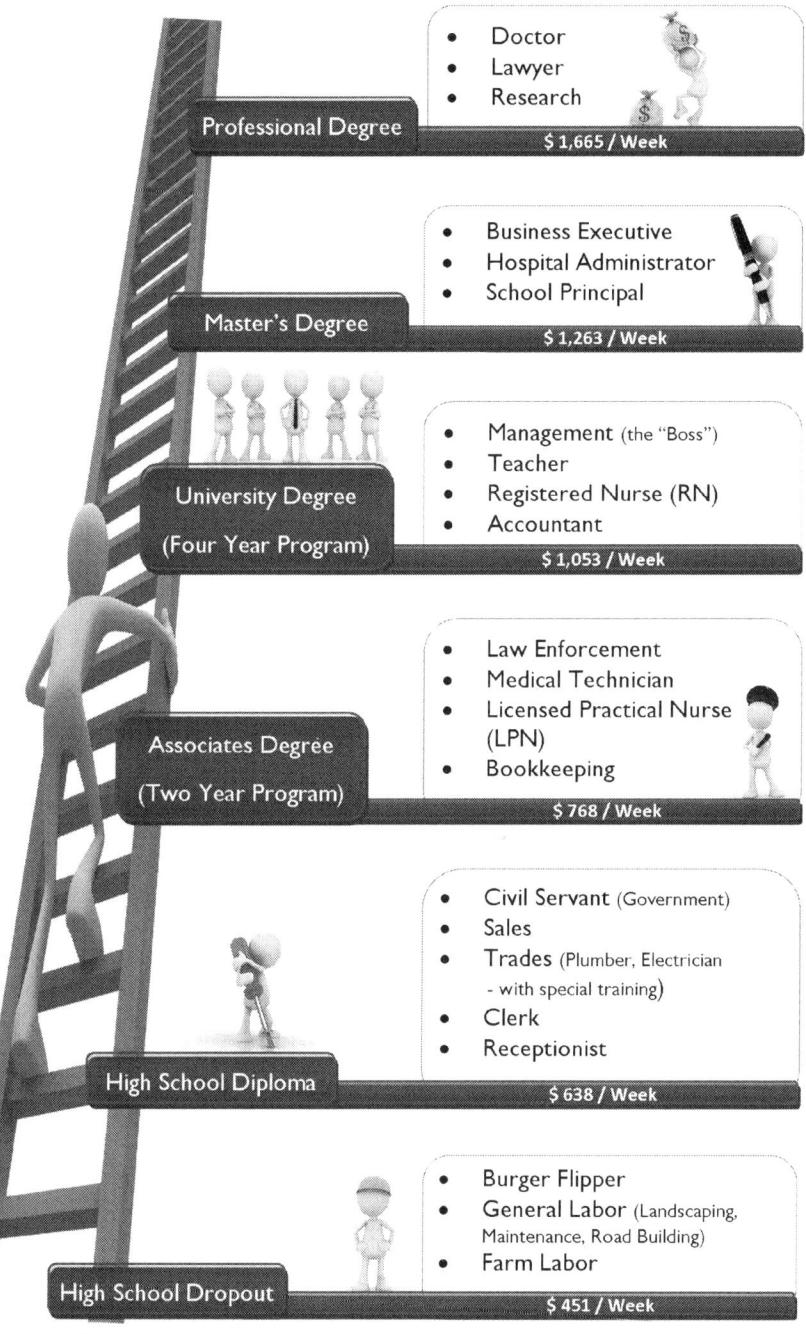

opportunities; opportunities bring income; so grades bring income. The title *Grades = Money* is not just a metaphor. It is a reality.

Conversely, just as surely as good grades create opportunities, underperformance in school limits them. Underperforming students may not say, "I want to work in a boring job" or "I want to be the first one laid off when the economy goes sour." They may not even understand the connection between grades and opportunity while they are in school. But the consequences eventually surface. College applications are rejected. Scholarship offers are non-existent. Job opportunities are few. Pay scales are low.

> Anyone who claims that money doesn't matter probably is not paying the bills, which describes most high school students.

Waiting until after leaving school may be too late. It is common for people who did not do well in high school to find themselves wishing they could go back and change their approach. But of course, this isn't possible. After graduation, high school is over. There is no second chance.

By the same token, it can be difficult for high school students to grasp the long-term impact grades have on the future. Going to a movie is more appealing than doing homework, and spending time gaming is more fun than studying for a test.

Movies and gaming are fun, homework and tests can be boring. Friends who are casual students can make it difficult to take school seriously, adding to the problem. Why bother?

Frankly, the immediate consequences for underperforming at school are few. Comments from teachers and parents that "you can do better" are easy to shrug off. But it is not a sign of weakness to agree with advice when the advice is correct. Doing well in school reflects maturity.

Earning good grades is worthwhile. With few exceptions, any student can earn good grades. It isn't difficult, it just takes skill. Once you know how to do it, earning good grades is easy. This book will show you how.

Understand the value of an education while you are still in school! Take a meaningful step toward self- reliance. Engage as an active learner and school will work for you, not against you.

The "education as a ladder" metaphor may seem obvious, but many students fail to understand it until it is too late. They may not realize how much education puts people ahead and how challenging life can be without one.

Are you ready to invest in your future? Do you have what it takes?

Take the quiz in the next chapter to find out.

Chapter 1: Key Points

- The real impact of school performance is not felt until after graduation.
- People with good grades and high academic achievement make more money.
- Education levels and academic performance determine a person's level in society.
- Understand the value of an education now, while you are still in school. Waiting until after leaving school may be too late.

"Unless a commitment is made, there are only promises and hopes; but no plans."
—Peter F. Drucker, business guru

CHAPTER 2
ARE YOU READY?
TAKE THIS QUIZ

This book is based on two assumptions:

1. Your grades are not as good as desired; and
2. You are willing to do something about it.

If both of these statements are true then this book can help.

The following quiz is designed to evaluate how your grades affect your self-image and how they affect the way others see you.

Some of the questions are quite personal and may be difficult to answer. Don't worry—it isn't necessary to share the results with anyone, and there are no "right" answers. Just think about each question and answer honestly. If the answer is in the middle between true and false, choose the answer that fits most of the time.

Results are discussed on the next page.

Self-Assessment Survey: Put an X in the column that most closely matches the statement.

#	Respond True or False	True	False
1	My grades accurately reflect my intelligence.	___	___
2	I enjoy going to school and find most courses interesting.	___	___
3	My parents are happy with my grades.	___	___
4	My teachers believe in me and encourage me to set my ambitions high.	___	___
5	I keep up with school and still have plenty of time to relax.	___	___
6	I am taking the most challenging courses offered for my grade.	___	___
7	People respect me—my friends, teachers, and parents alike.	___	___
8	I am self-motivated.	___	___
9	I feel in control of my life and like the direction it is heading.	___	___
10	School work seems to be easier for other people than it is for me.	___	___
	Count of responses for each column	___	___

INTERPRETING YOUR RESULTS

"False" answers to any of the first nine questions suggest that this book can significantly benefit your academic performance. This book teaches the Active Learning skills, and once you are an active learner, the answers to these questions will all be "true." Your confidence and self-worth will rise accordingly.

A "true" response to the last question—*School work seems to be easier for other people than it is for me*—is an indication of underdeveloped learning skills, which is what this book is all about. This is about to change for the better. Active Learning makes it easy to be a great student.

You may have noticed that the quiz does not ask, "Do you do your homework?" or "Do you study for tests?" Rather, it asks how your school performance impacts your self-worth and how others view you. School performance should not be the end goal but rather the means to the end. The end goals are confidence, self-worth, and opportunity.

If some of the survey questions arouse strong emotions then you are definitely ready to change. Emotional responses are an indication of frustration, which is a valid reaction to challenging situations. The comments below explain why students are often frustrated and how this book will help.

LEARNING IS A SKILL

Skills are different than talents and are *not* related to intelligence. Skills must be acquired. They are developed over time. You can be a great student regardless of your native "intelligence" (whatever that is).

Learning is often approached as a passive process. Come to class, listen to the teacher, and remember what sticks. But passive learning is not often effective. Most students need to engage in the material to really learn it.

Active Learning is a more effective approach to learning. Active Learning takes effort. It uses skills and techniques that make it easy to remember new information.

Learning is a skill, just like flying an airplane, playing an instrument, driving a car, or using technology are skills. Once you have the skills, it is easy to use them. If you want to see skills in action, contrast how an experienced driver maneuvers in heavy traffic compared to a new driver. The task is the same, but the execution can be very different.

Skills go beyond execution—they also affect learning. For example, young people generally adapt to new technology faster than their parents because they have better technical skills. People who understand computers have little difficulty learning to play new video games, but those who grew up without computers may never adapt.

Similarly, students who have developed good learning skills have little difficulty learning new course material. Their good techniques and competence as students make it easier to learn.

Most people assume that students will develop learning skills on their own. Unfortunately, this does not always occur. The result is that some students receive grades that are well below their potential. This can be frustrating for everyone—students, teachers, and parents alike.

It is especially frustrating for the student.

Skilled learners:

- Acquire new information quickly
- Retain new information permanently—not just for the test
- Do not struggle at school
- Do not allow challenging lessons to shake their self-confidence

Skilled learners are alert in class because they know how to make any subject interesting. They have a positive self-image because they see themselves as successful students and know that others regard them the same way.

HOW LEARNING HAPPENS

Scientists used to believe that our brains were pre-wired, and that learning occurred through the use and reinforcement of existing brain pathways. Development of new nerves (or pathways) was believed to be impossible after childhood.

We now know better. Our brains make new connections all the time. Learning creates new connections between brain cells and even generates new brain cells. This process has a technical name—"neuroplasticity"—which means "changing nerves."

Here is how it works: the first time we are introduced to something, the connections and pathways that processed the information are weak. The memory won't last unless the connections are reinforced. This is the basis for the old proverb "repetition is the mother of learning." Repetition creates long-term memory because it causes the connections between nerves to become stronger, making them permanent.

As with blazing a trail, new paths becomes easier to follow as they are used, and the more they are used, the more likely they are to remain accessible over long periods of time.

Learning is also reinforced by processing information using different parts of the brain. See it, hear it, say it, *and* write it down, then we are far more likely to learn something than if we just passively hear about it in a lecture. *Using multiple pathways promotes learning.*

Teaching is a particularly effective way to integrate new information. Being able to explain material requires understanding, retention, and description. Students who form study groups learn by teaching.

Active Learning exploits the science behind learning. That is why it is so effective.

CAUSES OF UNDERPERFORMANCE

Before launching into the techniques of Active Learning, it is important to ask yourself: why am I underperforming at school?

The word "underperforming" means *not doing as well as possible*. Not everyone can be at the top of the class, but everyone can and should perform to their potential. If not, they are underperforming.

For most students, underperformance can be attributed to a lack of commitment and to underdeveloped learning skills, as described above. But not every underperforming student has a problem with learning skills—the problem may lie elsewhere. It is always worth considering whether there may be an underlying condition that should be addressed. Examples include medical conditions, vision problems, dyslexia[i] (difficulty reading words and a tendency to confuse letters), learning disabilities, and problems at home. If you feel any of these conditions might be affecting your performance, seek help immediately. You are not alone, and there are people who want to help.

Poor performance often leads to negative reinforcement in the form of poor grades, criticism, and low expectations, which can reinforce negative attitudes and foster a culture of failure. Active Learning helps build positive attitudes and can break this cycle. But some students live in abusive environments, and, for them, the negative cycle may not originate with grades but tragically may be a result of the abuse. There are people and resources to intervene in such cases, too. Please seek them out if needed.

Similarly, students who suffer illness, who have poor diets, or who do not exercise may also have a physical component to their underperformance. For these students, the physical issues must be addressed before academic performance can improve. Hunger and low energy make learning difficult.

THE TRANSITION TO ACTIVE LEARNING

Active Learning improves grades and shows students how to study efficiently. Active learners are seldom bored. They experience less anxiety and feel better about themselves. Active learners have more opportunities offered to them, opportunities that underperforming students may not even know exist. Great students commonly live side by side with the underperformers but have very different experiences.

Most importantly, Active Learning gives students the confidence to take control of their futures. They create their own opportunities. Grades no longer limit opportunities. School is no longer a drag.

If you are underperforming at school, if you want to take control of your life, if you want to control how your life unfolds, if you want to stop being frustrated with your performance—then this book is for you.

Let's begin!

CHAPTER 2: KEY POINTS

- *Grades do not measure intelligence, but people use grades to judge performance. Good grades open doors, and poor grades close them.*
- *Grades can affect self-esteem and how you are viewed by others. If this is frustrating then it is time to do something about it.*
- *Underperforming students should be screened for medical and other conditions that may be affecting their grades.*
- *Learning is a skill that can be developed.*

"Luck is what happens when preparation meets opportunity."
—Seneca, first-century Roman philosopher

CHAPTER 3
THE FIVE TECHNIQUES OF ACTIVE LEARNING

The main Active Learning techniques can be summarized as follows:

1. Show up for class and come prepared.
2. Sit where the action is.
3. Write everything down.
4. Be sure you understand everything.
5. Read ahead.

Sounds simple, doesn't it? It can be.

It is helpful to understand the principles behind the techniques. Let us consider them in turn.

TECHNIQUE 1: SHOW UP FOR CLASS AND COME PREPARED

Most teachers make it impossible to earn a good grade without showing up for class. You may be thinking, *I have to show up. I'm in high school.* This is true, but showing up means being there mentally as well as physically. Showing up also means being well prepared.

Teachers often teach the same material year after year. They have seen many students go through the process; they know whether or not a student is in class—physically *and* mentally—and they take notice. Their perceptions affect how they grade—not just for participation, but also when deciding on how to mark a student who is at the borderline between two grades. If teachers know a student cares, they are more likely to give him or her the benefit of the doubt and the higher grade. If teachers feel the student doesn't care, they may not be so generous.

> **SKILL DEVELOPMENT TIP**
>
> *Do not attempt to change all your learning habits at once. Pick the skills that seem easiest and work to develop the others over time.*

"Being prepared" for class includes having completed the homework, done all the assignments, read ahead (discussed more below), and having everything needed to fully participate. Many underperforming students actually do their homework and then forget to hand it in! Nothing drags grades down like zeros for missed assignments.

Part of the Active Learning System is being organized, and step-by-step advice about how to become organized is provided in the next chapters. For now, keep in mind that one aspect of being organized means *making it impossible to forget*. Avoid the sinking feeling that comes when you realize that a homework assignment is at home sitting on the printer. Immediately after a homework assignment is completed, put it in a place (such as your backpack) where it cannot be left behind.

> **Make it impossible to forget!**
>
> *How can it be impossible to forget something? By establishing a routine and sticking to it. This can be as simple as putting homework assignments into a backpack as they are completed and putting the backpack by the door. Doing this guarantees that the homework won't be left behind in the morning.*

Being mentally present in class means not being fatigued. Set up a routine that provides for adequate sleep. Turn the cell phone off before going to bed to ensure a sound sleep without interruptions. Go to bed early enough to meet your body's needs, which is usually at least eight hours a night. Be sure to be rested on school days.

> SKILL DEVELOPMENT TIP
>
> *If you have a hard time waking up in the morning, you probably are not sleeping enough. Sleep is critical to learning. Listen to your body. Be sure to get enough sleep!*

It is also important to leave time for exercise. Exercise is essential to physical and psychological well-being, and it provides the energy needed to study effectively. As one Active Learner related, "I had some tough years when I wasn't doing very well academically, physically, or emotionally. What I have come to understand is that these three things can affect the others. Then I started working out, hard enough to make me sweat on a regular basis. I found that I was able to focus a lot better in class because I didn't have a bunch of built-up energy."

Food is extremely important. We are literally what we eat, so eating the right food makes has a big impact on how we feel and perform. Most high school students experience growth spurts, which can be accompanied by voracious appetites. This is the body's signal that it needs food. Oddly, many students skip breakfast, even though that is when the body most needs nutrition. Breakfast "breaks" the "fast" from sleeping overnight without food and fills the metaphorical fuel tank that the body needs for the day's activities. Be sure to leave time to eat breakfast every day and make sure the meal is nutritious. Candy bars and sodas do not qualify as nutritious breakfast food!

Show up prepared and ready to learn, both physically and mentally.

TECHNIQUE 2: SIT WHERE THE ACTION IS

Teaching in front of a room of students is a form of public speaking. Most public speakers tend to focus their attention on one part of the audience, and they use the people in that area to gauge their effectiveness. Eye contact, facial responses, and wandering attention all provide feedback, and good speakers use that feedback to help set their tempos. Speakers often direct their focus somewhere near the front of the audience. It may be in the center, off to one side, or a few rows from the front. In any case, speakers focus on people in the audience who are close enough to allow them to read facial expressions and establish eye contact.

Let us refer to that section of the audience as "where the action is." While this may not be the center seat of the front row, it is the center of the speaker's focus. Students who sit where the action is are virtually guaranteed to pay maximal attention throughout the entire class and will stay focused on the lecture.

Most people have difficulty staying focused for long periods of time. Their minds wander or they become bored or distracted. Being where the action is minimizes distractions. Having fewer people between the teacher and the student means having fewer opportunities to be distracted from what is being taught.

Try to maintain eye contact with the teacher. Maintaining eye contact commands his or her attention and conveys interest. This makes for a more direct and personal experience and improves retention.

A study at the University of California Los Angeles suggests that non-verbal body language accounts for much of our interpersonal communication.[ii, iii] Remain attentive and show interest—don't slouch, lean on elbows, listen to music, or stare at a laptop while the teacher is lecturing. Resist the temptation to text, check email, or pop into online social networking sites during class. Stay in the present; it will improve your retention. Stay focused on the class. Students who sit where the action is have a responsibility to engage. Live up to it!

> *If your friends give you a hard time about not sitting with them, explain that you hear better and see better near the front of the room. It will certainly be true.*

If the teacher has assigned seating away from the front, ask to be moved. Explain that you are having trouble following from further back. Don't lie—it isn't necessary. Everyone follows better from the front. It is only natural, and most teachers will be willing to oblige.

Sitting where the action is inevitably makes classes more interesting and class time seem to go by faster. It is one of the easiest ways to improve academic performance. Make it a habit.

TECHNIQUE 3: WRITE EVERYTHING DOWN

Whenever possible, try to write down everything that is presented during class. Taking notes makes it much easier to learn and remember new information.

Note-taking is hard work, so even if the material drags, writing notes keeps up the activity level and staves off fatigue. This is particularly important when sitting where the action is. The teacher will notice, and the student will benefit by not missing anything.

Writing information down also excludes potential distractions—whether from electronics, other people, or daydreams. Students who take notes are too busy to be distracted.

In some classes, teachers provide the material in a handout, often in the form of PowerPoint slides printed with one or two slides per page. If this is the case, follow along in the handout during class. Annotate the handout with highlights and comments to guide studying later on. Handouts can greatly facilitate note-taking, but do not assume everything mentioned

> *Note-taking improves retention. Writing something down after hearing it enlists more parts of the brain, which reinforces learning. Taking notes allows people to remember information more easily—simply by virtue of having written it down—even if the notes are never read. Taking notes requires "active listening" and is discussed in detail in Chapter 7.*

in class will be in the handout. Teachers routinely leave blanks where key points will be inserted to ensure that students listen in class. Be sure to fill in these sections during the lecture.

If your school provides materials in advance of class using one of the online services, print them out and review them *before class*. Note the sections where information is missing to ensure the information is captured during class.

Class notes provide a mental roadmap of the material presented in class. By the time the class ends, the materials will have been heard, processed, and written down (or highlighted). When the same notes are used to study later on, your brain will travel the same pathways that processed the information the first time. That is how we learn—by reinforcing connections and pathways in our brains. Because you have already heard the material and taken notes, the pathways are already established. Reviewing notes you created reinforces the material far more effectively than reading material created by someone else.

Good notes are a valuable resource, so students who take good notes often find they are very popular. Those who do not take good notes themselves may need help later on. Go ahead and share your notes (as long as it does not violate any policies). It can't hurt and may make the recipient more likely to help out if you need something later on.

There may be some teachers who don't want students to take notes, and there may be classes where taking notes is not practical. In these situations, a good substitute is to write a short summary of what happened in class later on that day. This can help to mentally recreate the semester when it comes time to study for the final exams. It will save time and effort and will improve recall. Taking notes reinforces learning.[iv]

Effective note-taking is an important skill that develops over time. Details are discussed in Chapter 7.

TECHNIQUE 4: BE SURE YOU UNDERSTAND EVERYTHING

Courses build on information like skyscrapers build floors on the ones below. It is essential to understand each lesson before starting the next one. Young children learn numbers before being taught how to add, they learn to add before learning to subtract, and they need both addition and subtraction in order to learn multiplication and division. The same can be said of history, higher-level math, science, English, and nearly every other subject.

New material can be challenging. Many students find it embarrassing to ask questions because asking questions reveals gaps in knowledge. Embarrassment is a real barrier to learning. If one student does not understand something then others probably do not, either. Knowing this can be empowering.

Of course, asking questions doesn't always mean interrupting class. It can mean circling a section in your notes and approaching the teacher after class or looking it up on the Web to see how other people explain it. Chances are that if the material prompted a question then someone on the Web has already researched it, written about it, published, and revised and updated articles about it. Learn from their experience while making use of your own resources.

> *Skill Development Tip*
>
> *As an active learner, never hesitate to ask questions when you don't understand something.*

It has often been said that there aren't any difficult subjects, just difficult teachers. Knowledge tends to be assembled from small bits of information. Even the most complex concepts are assembled from many simpler ideas. Yes, it can be intimidating when things appear to be complicated. But usually the material can be broken down into small, understandable pieces.

Students who don't understand something either missed important information that came before or the material hasn't been explained well. Always understand all of the material at every step before moving on to the next item. If something isn't clear then ask.

It is critical never to let something go by without understanding it. The next lesson (and the next and the next) may depend on it.

TECHNIQUE 5: READ AHEAD

Reading ahead provides such an advantage that it could almost be considered cheating. After all, students who read ahead know about the material before class has even begun. But reading ahead is not cheating. It is good strategy.

Reading ahead is another way to "be ready for class" as discussed above. Reading ahead:

- Makes the next day's class more productive. Students who read ahead come ready to learn and know in advance what they need to find out to understand the lesson.

- Provides a chance to plan what to ask about in class—or to bring up as an interesting point. Having intelligent questions demonstrates good preparation and a desire to learn.

- Makes the class time a review, not an introduction. Time will not be wasted trying to understand new concepts—they will already be familiar. Class will serve as a review that will help convert new material into long-term memory. By the time the class is over and the material has been written into notes and then studied again later for the final exam, it will have been learned and reinforced several times. This is how information is turned into knowledge.

These are the immediate benefits of reading ahead. There are also long-term benefits because, over time, others will take notice of your confidence and familiarity with the material and wonder how you always seem to know so much. This is very good. As with grades, being seen as the "smart one" can also become a self-fulfilling prophecy.

To put the concept of reading ahead into context, consider a study session where the math homework for Chapter 3.2 has just been completed. This is the best time to look ahead in the syllabus (or, in the absence of a syllabus, in the textbook) and scan the next section while the material is still fresh in mind from having just done the homework. A good approach would be to read through the introduction to the next section (3.3) and try a few of the problems at the end. If the homework is pre-assigned (syllabi do serve a purpose) or the assignments are published on the Internet, try doing tomorrow's homework today. Flag any problems that are difficult and plan to address them in class the next day.

It may seem counterintuitive, but students who take the time to read ahead actually spend less time doing homework than those who do not read ahead. I call this the "productivity paradox." A *paradox* is a truth that leads to a contradiction or a situation that defies intuition. Here, students who read ahead spend less time studying overall and retain the material better. Active learners encounter the productivity paradox time and time again as they develop their learning skills. The Active Learning System lets students spend less time studying and improves performance at the same time.

> *"I used to find one of the most challenging aspects of reading ahead to be retaining all of the new information for class time. But then I realized something: you are not expected to know any of the material beforehand. Hearing it in class really reinforced the information. Not to mention my friends thought I was a genius. It's like studying, without the extra time commitment!"*
>
> *- Lexi, an active learner*

Some subjects don't lend themselves to reading ahead. In that case, look up the material on the Web and see what others have written about it. In a creative writing class, for example, it might be helpful to look up similar courses and activities on the Internet. Chances are the teacher or professor used some of these same materials when preparing the class plans or lecture topics. A few minutes of preparation may anticipate the entire lesson.

Reading ahead is one of the most powerful techniques for improving your performance at school, yet it is one of the least practiced. Showing up to class knowing the day's lesson in advance creates a huge advantage. Everyone will recognize you as the smart student—and rightfully so.

ACTIVE LEARNING TECHNIQUES

These five techniques are the key building blocks to a successful academic experience. Think of each technique as a separate process. Develop them gradually and review your progress periodically. Pay attention to the impact they have on your learning progress over time.

Other considerations, such as time management, workspace design, study techniques, picking the right friends, and teacher relationships, are tools you can use to support these techniques and are explained in the next few chapters.

Chapter 3: Key Points

- There are five main techniques to the Active Learning System:
    1. Show up for class and come prepared. Have assignments ready to turn in. Be well rested, well fed, and show up on time.
    2. Sit where the action is. Maintain eye contact with the teacher whenever possible. Pay attention.
    3. Write everything down. Taking notes keeps you awake and makes it easier to remember new information.
    4. Be sure you understand everything. Ask questions if you do not, either during class or later on. Use your notes to highlight difficult concepts that need to be reviewed after class.
    5. Read ahead. This is not cheating but is good strategy. Reading ahead makes class a review and lets you listen more attentively. It also makes you appear smart.
- Develop these techniques gradually and review your progress over time. Although they seem simple, do not expect to master them overnight. These are serious skills that take time to develop. Enjoy the process and pay attention to how they make learning easier. Your appreciation of the benefits will increase your commitment to becoming an active learner.

Part 2

Create an Active Learning Culture

> "Control your destiny, or someone else will."
> —Jack Welsh, former CEO of General Electric

CHAPTER 4
TAKE CONTROL

The Active Learning techniques described in Chapter 3 provide a clear strategy for learning. They help structure an organized approach to school and are certain to improve academic performance. This chapter explains how to gain control over day-to-day activities and to make effective use of Active Learning skills.

Underachievers spend a great deal of time procrastinating and very little time producing. They can spend more time worrying about the work than it would take to do it. They may want the end result but may not be willing to put in the work to

> *The best way to de-clutter our environment is to take everything out and only put back things that we plan to use. Doing this with a closet can often create more room than we know what to do with—and generates bags of donations that the Salvation Army or Goodwill stores would be grateful to receive. If emptying a closet or deep-cleaning a room sounds daunting then chances are it is long overdue.*

make it possible. In other words, *underachievers do not control their lives very well.* They allow life to happen to them instead.

Similarly, many underperforming students manage their time poorly. They often worry about work rather than just doing it. They often engage in mind-numbing activities like gaming and television marathons. They sleep at odd hours and don't feel rested. They divide their attention among texting, music, and whatever else is going on. They are often bored.

Being organized is an example of the "productivity paradox" that was described in Chapter 3 and is an important part of Active Learning. Time spent organizing pays big dividends due to better time management.

FIRST, ORGANIZE YOUR SPACE

It is nearly impossible to perform well at school if the rest of one's life is a mess. It may seem that being organized takes too much time, but in the long run being organized saves a great deal of time. There are two aspects to organization: space and time. Let's first consider space.

"Space" encompasses the living environment—a bedroom, an entire house (even when living with parents or others), bureau, desk, car, and locker—all of the spaces that make up our world. These spaces should always be clean and organized. Keep things where they belong. De-clutter. If something has not been used in the past year, give it away or throw it away.

Untidy rooms are unsightly, but that isn't the real problem. Messy environments reduce productivity. People often say, "It's an organized mess. I know where everything is," but, in reality, disorganization limits effectiveness. The mess might involve a pair of dirty jeans that you wanted to wear this weekend but could not find beneath a pile of laundry, or "lost" items that really have been forgotten. Your piles of "stuff" are in the way. Clean up!

The same goes for computers. Computer file directories should be organized and regularly backed up. Are old files, photos, and music taking up disk space and making it difficult to find things? Archive them. De-clutter the computer desktop. Keep current files in a working directory and archive the rest. Subscribe to one of the free online storage services and store current files online. That way you can access them from anywhere.

Everything seems easier with a clean environment. Over time, being organized becomes less of a chore and more of a lifestyle. The small investment of time spent organizing creates significant efficiencies later on.

NEXT, CONTROL YOUR TIME

Organizing time is extremely important. It is amazing how much time can be wasted due to poor time management skills.

A key advantage of computerized and online calendars is that they can synch to your cell phone and provide reminders as you go through the day. Using your phone as a daily "list" of events can help to keep you on track.

Calendars and lists are keys to being organized. Paper calendars are fine and can be displayed on your bedroom wall or above your desk. If you have access to a personal computer, use it. Computerized calendars (such as the one found in Microsoft's Outlook, Google, or iCal) have several advantages over paper calendars: they set automatic alerts, prevent overlapping events, modify changes easily, prioritize activities, and categorize different occasions. The week of final exams, for instance, can be marked for high priority as well as color-coded to catch your attention.

Computerized calendars are also able to synchronize with your cell phone in order to provide you with audible, mobile reminders throughout the day. But do not make the mistake of relying solely on your cell phone calendar. Cell phones can be lost or malfunction. They should be used only as a convenience and not as a primary tool.

HOW TO SET UP A CALENDAR

It takes two steps to create an effective calendar. The first step is to set up important dates. The second is to schedule time around those dates.

Begin by entering the dates of major events throughout the year on the calendar, such as the first and last days of each semester, holidays, spring break, etc. Block out important dates to keep free, such as time for vacations. Be sure to ask family and friends if they are planning any special events or trips that need to be added.

Next, fill in the days for final exams, midterms, and the due dates of term papers and long-term projects. To avoid surprises, color-code these dates and set up a reminder to provide advance notice of when they are due. Add special dates for family events or activities that might limit the time available for studying. Some social events are

> **SKILL DEVELOPMENT TIP**
>
> *Controlling your time and organizing your space are not always possible. Some things cannot be controlled. Start with the big items—keep your desk organized, organize your calendar, and note the important events. Once these are under control, opportunities to go further will become obvious.*

more important than others, so use a color code to highlight the "must-attend" events versus the less important ones that could be displaced by studying, if needed.

Be sure to set target dates to complete major assignments several days before they are actually due. This provides time to review the work before handing it in and an opportunity to address any problems that need attention.

Some activities, like maintaining one's space (cleaning, doing laundry, shopping for groceries, etc.), must occur each week and can be set up as recurring events. It isn't necessary to note the micro-categories for these events on your main calendar. Not everything has to be planned, but do block a day or couple of hours in the week so you have time to complete them. Then be sure to use the time effectively so that regular chores and leisure do not infringe on work and social events.

USE YOUR CALENDAR TO SCHEDULE YOUR TIME

Conflicts immediately become apparent when setting up a calendar, such as having two term papers due in the same week or an important family event the week before finals. Use the calendar to plan around the conflicts. Spread work out to reduce stress.

Realistically, it may not be possible to predict exactly how much time studying, doing homework, and reading ahead will require, especially at first. To avoid overbooking, schedule work early in the day (perhaps once classes have finished) and allot a generous amount of time to complete it. Then allocate any extra time in the day for activities that you look forward to doing, such as exercise or watching a favorite television show. Building relaxation time into the schedule puts an effective time limit on the academic work and provides an incentive to stay on schedule.

> *Unforeseen scheduling conflicts become obvious with a calendar.*

If an assignment includes extensive reading, schedule it for when energy levels are high and when time is not rushed, such as over the weekend.

Never plan to cram. Cramming creates stress and stress is a barrier to long-term learning. Spread work out to span evenly over the semester. Unexpected assignments (and life) may impact schedules. Planning ahead can prevent being caught off-guard.

In particular, watch out for long-term assignments and term papers. These are usually assigned over long periods of time for a reason. They may require extensive reading, research into ongoing events, experiments, or personal interviews. Understand the reason for the long-term due date and plan for it.

If the course is designed such that the paper can be written at any time, begin writing it at the start or middle of the semester so it is taken care of early. This reduces stress later on and can provide familiarity with the course material in advance. This will be obvious to the teachers and will make the course easier to manage.

PLAN THE WORK AND WORK THE PLAN

Plan and update your calendar weekly. Make this part of your routine. Use this time to scope out the week's upcoming events and allocate time to do what needs to be accomplished. Sunday afternoons or evenings are ideal times to do this, before the week begins.

Use the planning sessions to strategize study schedules. For example, if there is an exam scheduled for Friday, plan to start reviewing the notes on Monday. Set aside a large block of time on Wednesday for a thorough review and a shorter one on Thursday for a refresher. Add brief sessions in between to reinforce the material, as time permits. By the time Friday comes around, the material will be very familiar. The repetition provides an opportunity for the brain to hard-wire the information—not only for the exam but for a lifetime.

The weekly calendar session can be used to anticipate and avert conflicts. Is there a big social event on the weekend and an exam on the following Monday? The exam might not have been part of this week's agenda, but calendar review made the conflict obvious. Schedule time on Friday and Saturday (of this week) to prepare for the exam. Knowing that the studying is done, the social event next Sunday will be more enjoyable. The exam on Monday will be manageable—without cramming.

A typical product of a calendar session is a "to-do" list for each day. Synch both the updated calendar and the to-do lists to your cell phone so they are always available, or alternatively just print them and keep them with you. They provide a roadmap of what needs to be accomplished each day. Following them ensures the work will be done on time, with time left over for relaxation.

BEING ORGANIZED IS EMPOWERING

This chapter is entitled "Take Control" because being organized provides the ability to be in control. Too many people let life happen to them and fail to plan (or even look) ahead. It is much easier and better to be organized.

Taking control often improves outlook. Yes, obligations continue. We still have to show up for school, do chores, study, and abide by the laws of society, but instead of feeling helpless and controlled by others, organized people own the process. By harnessing the time that might have been wasted on unproductive activities, control provides more time to do what is needed and more time to relax.

With control comes power. People will notice this and will be impressed by it. You will have more time to spend with others while still earning good grades. Parents, friends, and roommates will welcome the change to a cleaner, more organized space, a less stressed schedule, and a more relaxed atmosphere. They will be delighted when tasks are completed without asking and will be impressed when the work is done better and in less time than before. They will also be proud of your improvements at school.

Organization is essential to a high level of performance. In order to master Active Learning techniques, it is important to be organized.

Take control.

Chapter 4: Key Points

- *Being disorganized wastes time. Underperforming students are often disorganized.*
- *Organize your spaces (bedroom, the entire house, bureau, desk, car, and locker) and your time.*
- *Use free online services to store and organize files for school. This makes the files available from anywhere.*
- *Calendars should be used to anticipate events, conflicts, and time off.*
- *Use the Web to keep calendars current.*
- *Review and update your calendar weekly.*
- *Use the calendar to organize your daily schedule.*
- *Being organized puts you in control. Others will notice and appreciate the change.*
- *Take control!*

> "Be careful the environment you choose for it will shape you; be careful the friends you choose for you will become like them."
> —W. Clement Stone

CHAPTER 5
THE IMPORTANCE OF FRIENDS

High school is a very social time of life, and most high school students are influenced by the people around them. Friends take on very important roles as advisors, companions, and judges. Being popular can take on great importance.

Most high school students are influenced by those around them more than they would like to admit. Whether it is called peer pressure or herd mentality, it is a very real phenomenon. People who don't care about school, and who haven't "connected the dots" between their academic performance and their future, can drag a good student down. Surround yourself with people who do well in school and you will find that your grades will improve and your attitude toward school will become more positive.

DISTINGUISH BETWEEN FRIENDS AND ACQUAINTANCES

Relationships built around values endure longer than those built around convenience. Yet friends are often selected from among the people we see in our day-to-day lives. Friendships based on convenience may be common, but it is important not to confuse convenient acquaintances with true friendship. True friends share values, experiences, and growth.

Understanding friendships and the impact friends have is extremely important. Friends influence performance and choices. Having the right friends can make all the difference in achieving success.

Imagine a high school junior thinking about applying for college or university. This can be a stressful process. It may involve enrolling in SAT preparation courses, strategizing reference and recommendation letters, working on essays, working on grades, and touring college campuses.

Spending time with students who are going through the same process will make it easier than trying to manage these challenges out of context. The "college prep" group may not have lunch together and may not be in the same activities after school, but they share similar goals and aspirations. They can support each other through the process.

The same can be said for studying. Students with friends who are doing well in school find it much easier to stay focused than students who have friends that are underperforming. By all means enjoy the company of soccer friends during practice, but spend quality time with people who are going places. Success is contagious.

Conversely, failure can also be contagious. "Friends" who would have you skip assignments

> *Consider Jake, for example. Jake is a freshman who is bored one evening and wants to order pizza with a friend. He can call either his football buddy to watch ESPN or his biology lab partner to review for next week's test. If he calls his football buddy, they will likely spend the entire night discussing sports. If he calls his lab partner, they will still be able to check on the game but will mostly focus on studying for the upcoming test. By choosing the study option, Jake may even find he forms a new bond around sports with his lab partner. They will have more to talk about in the future and will have contributed something positive to each other's lives. But spending the night with his football buddy won't contribute anything and won't help his performance at school. It will only lead to the same old conversation the next day about the game's highlights.*

for an evening out do not have your interests in mind. Anyone who would compromise your grades is not a friend. They may not be consciously malicious, but they are causing harm nevertheless.

> The best friendships have synergy. Synergy exists when the whole is greater than the sum of the parts. Good friends bring out the best in each other and make the other person better than they would be if they were not in the friendship. Synergistic friendships usually develop from common interests and true concern for the other's well-being. It doesn't often happen while watching TV. It does happen when you learn from each other and help each other through challenging times.

Find ways to make learning enjoyable. Find friends with similar interests to form study groups. Celebrate high exam scores and good grades. Abandon negative attitudes about school and allow yourself to enjoy learning. Engage in the process—the more you do, the more enjoyable it will become.

Understand that friendships change over time. It is natural for friendships to change depending on circumstances. New schools, new towns, new jobs, marriage, new interests, and many other changes can bring new friends. Friends from high school often go in completely different directions once college starts and may drift apart.

SEEK OUT FRIENDS BASED ON SHARED INTERESTS

The friends we choose at every stage in the educational process should be people who share our values for high performance at school.

Successful people value achievement in others and usually surround themselves with other successful people. The people you would like to be around may not welcome you into their circle unless you have something to offer. Sometimes it may be necessary to offer more than just a winning personality and high academic dreams. Find common interests like music, hobbies, skiing, snowboarding, or paintballing—smart people don't just read books all day. In fact, the opposite is often true. Good students have time to enjoy other activities because they use Active Learning techniques, whether or not they have read this book. Try organizing an activity and invite interesting people to attend. Whatever the activity is, taking the initiative to make things happen will cause people to want to be included.

> "Keep away from people who try to belittle your ambitions. Small people always do that, but the really great make you feel that you, too, can become great."
>
> —Mark Twain

Another tip: it can be very helpful to spend time with people who are a year ahead in school. It isn't cheating to have friends who have already taken the courses you are taking now. They can provide valuable insights and suggest tactics about how to study and prepare. Even if you do not become close friends, become familiar enough that you are able to ask for advice. Don't be tempted to copy their papers or cheat—that is neither necessary nor helpful. But do ask what works with which teachers as you develop strategies for success.

Some schools provide mentoring opportunities. Consider identifying a mentor if one is available. Friends can serve as mentors, too. This can go both ways—offering to mentor someone who is struggling may reap benefits later on.

Chapter 5: Key Points

- *Friends share common interests. Acquaintances share common schedules.*
- *Friends can make a huge difference in your performance at school, both positively and negatively.*
- *The friends we choose should be people who share our values for high performance at school.*
- *Students who are a year ahead can provide valuable advice for success.*
- *Taking the initiative to make things happen will cause people to want to be around you.*

"Our attitude toward life determines life's attitude towards us."
—*Earl Nightingale*

CHAPTER 6
TEACHERS

Teachers are central to the student experience, and knowing how to interact positively with teachers can be very valuable.

Successful students know how to bring out the best in good teachers and how to avoid the worst in bad ones.

It is easy for students to think of teachers as institutions rather than as people. But teachers are people, with unique personalities, levels of caring, and different abilities.

Most students can identify some teachers who were great and others who were not so great. It does not matter. Students cannot afford to allow their teachers—whether great or mediocre—to limit their success. Instead, active learners take control of their own education and find ways to work with any teacher to achieve their goals.

MANAGING TEACHER PERCEPTIONS

> ### SKILL DEVELOPMENT TIP
>
> *Understanding teachers as people and not only as functionaries is an important step in establishing a positive relationship. Try to establish eye contact with the teacher during class. This can help you to stay focused and also lets the teacher know you are paying attention. You may be surprised at how much teachers struggle to engage students. A well-timed smile or nod of the head from an attentive student can mean a great deal to a teacher during a difficult lesson.*

As with most people, first impressions can have a significant impact on how teachers come to view students later on. Teachers often label students, and this becomes their identity. The "lazy" one, the "bright" one, the "rude" one, the "smart" one, the "dumb" one—the title may not be accurate, but it describes how students are perceived by their teachers. It is important to make the initial impression a positive one because negative first impressions can become a lasting handicap.

The easiest way to create a positive first impression is to show up for your first classes prepared and ready to learn.

The school schedule may not start until the first day of the semester, but a successful student's work begins well before then. This means reading ahead throughout the week prior to starting class. Look up information about the class on the Internet. Talk to students who had the teacher last semester or last year. Time spent preparing will be time well spent.

As we discussed in Chapter 3, the subliminal messages sent during class can have a big impact on what teachers think of their students as individuals. Sit where the action is, make eye contact, and take notes. Stay alert.

The quality of a student's work also sends a loud message to the teacher about how seriously he or she is approaching a class. Work should be well presented. Neat, clean, organized assignments broadcast a serious effort while sloppy, incomplete work says, "I don't care." Teachers recognize talent, so show them talent. They will respond accordingly.

Some teachers are sticklers for format, and formats may differ among teachers. Deal with it. Don't lose points over formatting and don't try to fight the system. Instead, master the system. Make it work for you. There will be plenty of time to change the world later on. Students must try to conform.

Don't be a sycophant (brown-nose). Nobody respects that. There is a difference between being prepared and being a sycophant. Be respectful and courteous but avoid the temptation to butter up the teacher just to score points. This tactic won't impress most teachers.

Above all, it is imperative that the teacher understands you are a serious student. Approach both the class and the teacher with a professional attitude. Remember, school is an academic setting where students learn new material and hopefully earn good grades. Study hard for tests even if the material seems to be under control. Review assignments with teachers if the scores are low. Let them know it matters to you.

Make it *impossible* for teachers to dismiss you as just another student. Be ready to learn and they will be challenged to teach. Do not try to be their friend but do earn their respect. Use Active Learning techniques and you will.

THE TEACHING CAREER CYCLE

Students will encounter many teachers over their academic career, and *vice versa*. In addition to understanding why people teach, it is helpful to assess where teachers are in the career cycle. Understanding where a teacher is psychologically can help determine which strategy to use in his or her class.

While there are certainly exceptions, a teaching career often follows a pattern that begins with hope and idealism and ends in fatigue. There is no set time for this cycle to occur. Some teachers burn out after one year. Others never lose their positivity.

Let the idealists know how much they are appreciated. Be sure they realize the impact they are having. Skip that message for the teachers who have reached the burnout stage of their careers. With these teachers, the goal is to make their lives as simple as possible and avoid causing problems.

In any event, it is worthwhile to take time to understand your teachers. Identify their motivations and respond to them appropriately. Do all you can to develop effective teacher-student interactions. Successful students depersonalize their feelings about teachers and approach them as professionals.

WORK THE SYSTEM

Never forget that as the front line of the school experience, teachers stand between students and their goals. Teachers may decide to be an obstacle or a bridge, or both. Work with them in a positive way and do not let their idiosyncrasies stand in the way.

In class, adhere to the old adage that "the teacher is always right." Question teachers and comment on interesting perspectives, but never accuse a teacher of being wrong during class and never try to take over a lesson. Realistically, it is far more likely that the teacher is correct since the material is very familiar and, politically, it is never helpful to embarrass a teacher. Resist the temptation to grandstand out of a desire to look good to your peers.

No matter how idealistic or tired, enthusiastic or lazy, excited or burnt out, teachers have to use some sort of objective criteria upon which to judge performance. These may include standardized tests, homework credit, or participation points. Regardless of the criteria, students should understand what is expected from the very first day of class. Most teachers publish a syllabus for their classes. If the grading information isn't offered, ask for it. Set up a strategy to meet all of their requirements from day one.

The distribution of points in a teacher's grading system reflects his or her priorities. This should send a clear message as to how to plan to spend your time before each class, i.e., how to set up the calendar. For example, if a term paper is worth 50 percent of a history grade then plan to spend about half the semester's "history" time to work on the term paper and start the work as soon as possible. If classroom participation counts toward the grade then make a point to prepare an intelligent question or comment to bring up in each class. This won't happen naturally. It should be part of the "reading ahead" process discussed in Chapter 3.

TEACHER RELATIONSHIPS

Never think of teachers as friends. Teachers are not your friends. Some will act like friends but they invariably fall back into their professional role as the course progresses (usually around final exam time or when grades are being given). From the teacher's perspective, students come and go and they will have a new batch next year. Students are a very temporary part of a teacher's life.

Students can be surprised when they run into a teacher at a grocery store two or three years after they completed their class and the teacher has no idea who they are. This should not seem strange. The teacher may have taught hundreds of students during that time. In addition, the physical changes that students undergo during high school can make them difficult to recognize years later!

Of course, it isn't always this way. You may develop a student-teacher bond with some teachers that may last forever, especially if you are an active learner and your interest validates the teacher's professional choice. But understand that even with the strongest student-teacher bonds, teachers encounter many students each year. What goes in one year may be pushed out the next. It is not personal; it is simply the reality of working with so many people each year.

Active learners do well with any teacher because they take the primary responsibility for their education. When active learners work with great teachers, the interaction can be very rewarding for both the student and the teacher. Books provide the essential information and teachers provide context to make it meaningful. They explain, interpret, discuss, and expand on the material, and great teachers make the lessons come alive.

Enjoy your teachers. Bring out the best in them, so they can bring out the best in you.

Chapter 6: Key Points

- Teachers are people, not institutions.
- Teaching is just one aspect of a teacher's job.
- It is worthwhile to understand teachers as people and treat them according to their motivations, career stages, and expectations.
- First impressions can have lasting effects. Use Active Learning techniques to create positive first impressions.
- Use the syllabus and point distribution as a guide to understand the teacher's priorities in the class.
- Active learners can bring out the best in teachers to create a win-win situation.

Part 3

Advanced Active Learning Techniques

"Know how to listen, and you will profit even from those who talk badly."
—Plutarch (Greek priest and philosopher, first century AD)

CHAPTER 7
ACTIVE LISTENING

It can be challenging to listen attentively. Minds wander. Distractions can cause us to lose focus. It is common to tune back in to a lecture only to find that what was being said for the last five minutes was completely missed.

Failure to listen attentively wastes time and creates more work later on. The goals of Active Learning are to retain information for the long term, to make great grades, and to spend as little time as possible doing it. Students are required to attend class. Why not tune in and make the most of the time?

What is the best way to do this? The answer is the Active Learning technique called a*ctive listening.*

For this discussion, "active listening" is defined as the combination of listening, processing, and recording information while hearing it rather than simply following what is being said. Active listening wards off boredom—even if the information is bland—because it brings the listener into the process.

> S*KILL* D*EVELOPMENT* T*IP*
>
> *Practice active listening both in class and in everyday life. See how often you can repeat back what you just heard in conversation. It should be easy if you listen actively. If not, chances are you are thinking and not listening and need to work on your listening skills!*

Active listening takes a significant amount of effort, which serves to keep the listener alert and interested.

The technique is simple. It begins by being prepared for class and arriving ready to listen. This means being rested, well-fed, and maybe having exercised to be fully alert (recall the discussion about personal management and scheduling from Chapter 4). It is important to sit "where the action is." Minimize distractions—turn off cell phones, music devices, and other electronics. Put aside thoughts about outside activities so you can focus on the material. Have a notebook or laptop ready to start taking notes. Establish eye contact with the teacher and renew this connection several times during the class in order to broadcast your interest in what is being said.

Do this every time you come to class.

Contrast this approach to learning with what underperforming students often do.

Underperforming students often arrive to class half-asleep and unfocused. They may enter at the last minute and sit near a friend rather than front and center. They may avoid engaging in classwork for as long as possible. Instead of listening, they may spend class texting friends and making arrangements for later activities.

Keys to Active Listening.

Arrive fresh, rested, fed, and alert.

Remove distractions: cell phones, music devices, etc.

Sit where the action is. Establish eye contact with the speaker and use facial expressions to communicate your interest (nods, frowns, etc.).

Focus. Block out wandering thoughts and tune in to the topic at hand.

Set up your notes so they are organized. This includes the date, topic, teacher/speaker name, page references, etc.

Take organized notes. If the class slides are provided in a handout, take notes on the handout.

Supplement notes with added references later on.

File the notes in an organized notebook or computer directory so they can be efficiently reviewed later.

These students are clearly not actively listening. The difference is obvious. So are the results.

TAKING NOTES REINFORCES WHAT YOU HEAR

Notes play a key role in active listening. To start, set up a notepad or a file on the laptop with a clearly titled and dated document. The notes will be used for studying, so keep them neat and organized. Keep notes for different classes in separate binders or in their own computer directories/folders.

The title should include the class, the date, and the name of the speaker. Use the lecture topic as the title. Add a reference to the assigned reading to make it easy to look up information later.

Note-taking is a skill and it may not come naturally at first. The challenge is to be able to listen and take notes at the same time. This takes some practice. Start with short phrases and key words. Write during pauses in the lecture. Do not try to capture every word like a court room transcriptionist; instead capture thoughts and themes. Write down key points and especially highlight what will be needed for the test. Listening is the priority so listen attentively and write once the concepts are clearly in mind. Over time, the writing will come automatically.

Handouts greatly facilitate note-taking. If the handout follows the lecture, use it as the template for your notes. Some teachers provide handouts of the PowerPoint slides used in the lecture. If this is the case, mark them up with your own comments, observations, and prompts for later review. Always highlight points that are emphasized in class. Fill in any missing information. Use the handout to anticipate what will be discussed next and be prepared to participate in the discussions.

Class notes do not have to be written in complete sentences. Leave the final formatting to later. With that said, some details can be important—so do write down examples and important commentary. A few key words can prompt recall later on, when studying for exams.

Developing a shorthand system can make reviewing class notes easier to follow. For example, use an asterisk to highlight items that the teacher indicates will be on the test. Use arrows to indicate that you need to look something up and question marks to indicate material that went by too quickly to absorb. Well-structured notes do not only summarize information. They also serve as a study guide.

I find that the best way to take notes is in outline format. Teachers typically organize lectures using outlines so that the information flows clearly. I once approached a professor with a question after class and showed him the section in my notes where I had a question. He saw my notes, gave me a funny look, and opened his notebook to his own lecture notes. The two outlines—the professor's and mine—were virtually identical.

> ### Skill Development Tip
>
> *Active listening is a critical part of being an active learner. It prevents wasting class time and greatly improves retention. It takes no extra time and is one of the most effective Active Learning techniques.*

A sample of notes from a lecture on the Cuban Missile Crisis is provided later in this chapter. Use them as a guide, not as a template! Everyone develops his or her own style.

Note-taking skills improve over time. A good rule of thumb is that notes are effective if the student could give the lecture using the notes after class.

ACTIVE LISTENING SAVES TIME LATER

The benefits of active listening are evident:

- It keeps you awake.
- It makes the class more interesting (and go by faster).
- It ensures that you will hear and process the information as you hear it.
- It accelerates learning.
- It saves time when you need to study for the exam.

Resist the temptation to treat class lectures as entertainment. Passive listening is temporary. Active listening causes you to participate and improves recall. Having good notes can save many hours of work when it comes time to review the material. Reading your own notes is like reliving the lecture. As a result, an entire semester's material can be reviewed in a short period of time.

Students who listen actively in class tend to be better listeners in their personal lives, as well. They pay attention to what is being said and do not allow their minds to wander. Other people appreciate this and come to view active listeners as intelligent, aware individuals.

Because they are.

> *Active listening takes advantage of the neuroplasticity concepts described in Chapter 2. Writing and listening use different parts of the brain. Writing down information that was just heard reinforces the formation of new neural connections, which helps to store the information in long-term memory. Later, when referring back to the class notes to study, multiple neural pathways are used to reprocess the information, further committing it to long-term memory.*

Sample notes from a class in American history on the Cuban Missile Crisis are provided on the next page. They consist mostly of short phrases and are in outline format. Most teachers use outlines to organize their lectures, making this a natural format to use when taking notes.

Symbols are used as shorthand to highlight certain items with special emphasis:

***   This symbol marks items the teacher indicated will be on the test.

=> LU   This is a prompt to look up more information about the item.

?   Question marks indicate a need for further study or clarification.

American History - 10/14/20xx   Mr. Bates
The Cuban Missile Crisis

I. General Info
    a. AKA *The October Crisis*
         i. Russians called it the *Caribbean Crisis*
    b. USSR v. USA played out in Cuba
    c. John F. Kennedy was president
         i. NSA was McGeorge Bundy / Sec Defense was Robert McNamara
    d. Russia tried to put missiles in Cuba – could have hit the US   (=> LU: How far is the US from Cuba?)

II. Weapons
    a. "Medium and intermediate range ballistic nuclear missiles" – (MRBM's and IRBM's) ***
    b. Could reach most of US / short warning

III. Start
    a. US suspected missile factories in August, 1962
        i. Russian fighter jets spotted "MiG's" ***
    b. 10/14/1962 – a US "U-2 photoreconnaissance" airplane – high altitude – took photos of bases and missiles
    c. Considered several responses
        i. "Do nothing" / full military action / diplomacy / attack missiles, etc.

IV. Politics
    a. Followed failed "Bay of Pigs" invasion in April 1961 (US invaded Cuba) => LU
    b. Going on during the Berlin blockade => LU / Cold war
    c. US had more missiles than Russia at the time, more subs
    d. US put in naval blockade
    e. "Nikita Khrushchev" *** KNOW NAME *** Soviet premier – said this would "propel humankind into the abyss of a world nuclear-missile war"
    f. Was very intense – international response – China sided with Cuba
    g. Raised alert level (? What are alert levels? Is this Defcon?)
    h. *** Adlai Stevenson was UN rep for the US
    i. Several blockade encounters / US nearly launched attack / Alert level raised / 510 war planes were ready to go from Florida
    j. Soviet sub nearly launched nuke (US learned this after the crisis)

V. Resolution
    a. October 28, 1962 ***
    b. UN Secretary General U.Thant / Kennedy / Khrushchev made a deal
        i. USSR removes missiles ***
        ii. US promises never to invade Cuba ***
        iii. "Kennedy-Khrushchev Pact" *** KNOW TERMS
    c. Missiles removed

VI. Long-term effects
    a. Created "hot line" direct phone between Moscow and DC
    b. Kennedy-Khrushchev Pact helped Castro, guaranteed US would not invade Cuba

Chapter 7: Key Points

- Active listening involves listening, processing, and recording information while hearing it.
- Active listening takes no more time than passive listening but saves a great deal of time when studying.
- Take notes in outline form and develop your own shorthand format to guide studying later on.
- Keep notes neat and organized.
- Benefits of active listening go beyond the classroom.

> "There is more treasure in books than in all the pirate's loot on Treasure Island."
> —Walt Disney

CHAPTER 8
ACTIVE READING

Anyone who has read this book to this point clearly knows how to read. The question is, how well? Could your reading style best be described as "skimming"? Is it a "check the box" exercise done at someone else's request? Or was the material being absorbed, reflected upon, and related to practical applications and academic performance?

Plowing through a book without reflecting on the material it contains is passive reading. Absorbing the material and relating it to academic performance is active reading.

Active reading is a powerful tool in the Active Learning process. It takes more effort than passive reading but it greatly improves retention because you actively participate in the process. As with active listening, active reading staves off boredom, and time seems to pass much more quickly.

> *Skill Development Tip*
>
> *Most books and articles are divided into cohesive sections. Take advantage of this organization when you read. Try not to leave a book in the middle of a chapter, and before you resume reading after a break, take time to recall what you read before launching into the next section. If you cannot recall what was read, you may as well have not read it!*

Active reading involves recalling the material during the process to ensure that the information is committed to memory. The process is similar to blazing a trail. The more times a trail is used, the more permanent it becomes.

Active reading also triggers associations between new and familiar concepts. This happens automatically as the brain links what we already know to new material being read.

Many articles have been published about active reading. Some of them are complicated and can be difficult to follow. The active reading approach presented here is simple and easy to master. It involves these five steps:

1. Skim the material.

2. Ask questions.
3. Read effectively.
4. Recite key points to confirm retention.
5. Review what was read.

Let's review each of these steps to see what's involved.

STEP 1: SKIM THE MATERIAL

The first step in active reading is to gain a general understanding of what is about to be read in order to direct the focus to the important areas.

Consider a reading assignment in a chemistry course. The teacher assigned a chapter on a new topic called stoichiometry (balancing chemical equations) with equations to memorize and specific concepts to retain. "Skimming" the chapter involves looking over the section headings and evaluating how much of the material is new, versus how much is already familiar, and estimating the time it will take to read through the material. The estimates become incorporated into the study session plan. Having an overview of the material and a sense of the time it will take to read it will make the reading more efficient. (Study sessions and study plans are covered in the next chapter. They provide the structure needed to reduce the time needed to study.)

In another course, the English literature teacher assigns a novel to read by next Friday. Skim through the novel and browse the Web for information about the theme, hero, protagonist, and other basic information. Having this information in mind—even before opening the book—will help focus the reading on the key issues. It may also reveal conflicting opinions or controversies about the material that may be brought up in class discussions. Being aware of these controversies before reading the novel will help discern the issues and will improve understanding of the material.

Skimming the material makes reading more efficient. Just as it would be unwise to set out on a journey without knowing the destination so, too, is it unwise to start a reading assignment without knowing where it will take you.

STEP 2: ASK QUESTIONS

The skimming process can be intriguing. New vocabulary, new concepts, and new issues may become obvious. Make a list of the new material in your notes. Use the list to guide your focus as you read. If certain words or topics prompt questions, write the questions down so you can come back to them later. They may provide the basis for questions you raise in class or lead you to review material from a prior course that was related to the current topic.

You will incorporate these questions into your review after you have finished reading (below). The more times the new topics are considered, the more likely they are to become part of your permanent memory.

STEP 3: READ EFFECTIVELY

To read effectively, you must be able to concentrate. Some people are able to block out distractions without isolating themselves, but many cannot. Make it easy. Find a quiet space to read that eliminates distractions and prevents interruptions.

It cannot be over-emphasized how important it is to read without interruptions. Turn off your cell phone. We learn most efficiently when we enter a condition known as an *alpha state*. An alpha state occurs when we are relaxed, focused, and aware—the combination of these emotions incurs a pattern of brainwaves known as *alpha waves*. These waves are slower than theta waves (which are the predominant patterns in your brain during normal waking activity) and occur during times of pure concentration. Alpha waves trigger increased activity of some parts of the brain—in particular, the visual cortex (the part associated with vision). This permits the brain to visualize the material and reinforces learning. Alpha states may also inhibit extraneous brain activity, commonly referred to as "daydreams."

Anyone who has read a book, watched a movie, or focused on a task only to notice that more time has gone by than realized has experienced an alpha state. As we concentrate, our brain becomes fully absorbed in an activity. It sets off an internal signal to slow down unrelated activities and an alpha state ensues. This trance-like alpha state allows the brain to focus entirely on the material at hand.

Learning occurs very efficiently in an alpha state. It is the optimal condition for reading. Total attention must be focused in order to enter an alpha state. Avoid all distractions—human, animal, and electronic—when you read.

STEP 4: CONFIRM YOUR RETENTION

Active reading requires the reader to participate aggressively in the reading process to recall what was just read. There are two recall components to the active reading process: immediate and long term. Immediate recall is done each time a page is turned. Long-term recall is exercised as each section is completed.

IMMEDIATE RECALL

Immediate recall is primarily used for non-fiction assignments such as history, science, and math. It is used to commit facts and details to long-term memory.

Most books are printed with facing pages, so turning a page advances the book two pages at a time. Each time a page is turned, pause to recall the key points from the previous

Active Reading

two pages. *Without turning back*, jot down the points in note form. The notes should be neat—they will be used later to study. Writing recruits different parts of the brain than those used for reading. Processing information in multiple pathways promotes retention. Note the page numbers to allow for later reference.

After listing the key points, flip the page back to confirm that the notes captured the material accurately. Review the questions and vocabulary that you noted earlier to be sure you understand them. After correcting any errors and filling in any missing details, continue reading. With practice, this process should take only thirty to sixty seconds for each turned page. It saves a great deal of time later on.

LONG-TERM RECALL

Long-term recall occurs as reading progresses and can be used for both non-fiction and fiction assignments. After completing each section, or the entire chapter, pause and recite (mentally or aloud) the key points from the material. Compare your recall to your notes rather than the original text whenever possible.

Long-term recall helps solidify information and re-engages with the notes. Doing this significantly reinforces memory.

To summarize, the reading portion of active reading involves reading two pages, pausing for immediate recall, noting key points, finishing a chapter or section, confirming long-term recall, and continuing on. An active reader should spend about 80 percent of the time reading and 20 percent of the time in the recall process. When the reading is done, the material will be well on its way to being hard-wired into permanent memory.

The active reading process becomes much quicker as you master it and is *extremely* effective.

An active reader might pause now to review the notes for the last few pages. They might look something like this:

Ch. 8: Active Reading / Pages 24–45

1. Active reading improves retention
2. 5 Steps: Skim / ask questions / read effectively / confirm retention / review

   a. Skim
      - Page through it, look up Web summaries, know what is involved
   b. Ask Questions – Make a list of new concepts
   c. Read Effectively
      - Quiet space, no cell phone
      - Achieve "alpha state" – get immersed in the material
   d. Confirm Retention
      - Immediate: Turn page, take notes, check accuracy, and correct as needed
      - "Long Term": Recall again and review notes at end of section or chapter
   e. Review

[The readers' notes will continue from here]

STEP 5: REVIEW WHAT WAS READ

The last step of active reading is to review the entire material that was read. The review process is similar to the "skimming" process in Step One. With textbooks, the review might involve looking back at section headings to recall the major points, similar to the process described as long-term recall but for the entire reading. Use this time to review what others may have said about the material online and compare their comments to your own notes.

Some textbooks list key points or provide summary sections at the end of each chapter. These can be very helpful. Be sure to review them carefully and check what is listed against your own recall of the material. Use the list to reinforce your memory, both at the time and later on when studying for an exam. (You may have noticed the chapter summaries that follow each chapter in this book. They are meant to promote active reading.)

The review should take only a few minutes, but it really helps to improve retention. If the assignment is a long one that was divided into several sessions, read over the notes from prior reading sessions at this point. Eventually the material will become so familiar that the reviews will seem to be pre- programmed.

Do you remember the trail metaphor from the beginning of this chapter? Active reading is like blazing a trail. Frequent passage keeps weeds from growing!

ACTIVE READING MAY TAKE LONGER BUT IT SAVES TIME OVERALL

When done correctly, active reading can take less time *overall* than passive reading. This may seem counter- intuitive, but it is true for three basic reasons:

1. Active reading organizes the work (Step One) and helps us to concentrate (because the brain is induced into an alpha state)—both of which cause us to read faster and more efficiently.

2. After reading using the active reading technique, it is unlikely that you will have to read the material again.

3. The alpha state that is achieved during active reading makes time pass very quickly. Even though active reading may take the same amount of time as passive reading, time *seems* to go by much faster than it does when half-heartedly plodding through the material.

The material has to be read at some point. Why not be efficient? Incorporate active reading techniques, and your academic performance will immediately benefit.

CHAPTER 8: KEY POINTS

- Active reading engages the reader and improves retention.
- There are five steps to active reading:
  1. Skim the material— preview it; look up Internet references and summaries.
  2. Ask questions and make a list of new concepts.
  3. Read effectively. Avoid distractions. Try to achieve an alpha state, which occurs when the brain is focused and learning efficiently.
  4. Confirm retention every two pages and at the end of major sections and chapters. Make notes that summarize key points.
  5. Review the entire reading. Compare your notes against the chapter summaries.
- Notes from active reading sessions should be used to study for exams.
- Active reading promotes recall and reduces overall studying time.

> *"Ordinary people think merely of spending time. Great people think of using it."*
> —Author unknown

CHAPTER 9
ACTIVE STUDYING

Studying and exercising have much in common. The thought of exercising is often unpleasant, while actually doing it feels good. The reason people seldom say, "I wish I did not exercise" after a good workout is because they feel better for having done it.

Studying is the same way. The most difficult part tends to be sitting down to start. After that, studying tends to be interesting and enjoyable.

Underperforming students may not appreciate the benefits of studying. Quite realistically, their study skills may be such that the benefits are not clear. Studying may take up too much time because the study sessions were not well organized.

> ### Skill Development Tip
>
> *Teaching is often the best way to learn. Reinforce your study time by explaining what you learned to a classmate or family member. Make the subject interesting by relating it to current events or familiar topics. Be sure you can explain the material by actually trying to do so. If you can explain it, you are guaranteed to understand it.*

Studying is often what turns underperforming students into great students. Reviewing material, completing assignments, and reading ahead provide a great advantage to any student. Many students underestimate the importance of homework because the contribution of homework to the overall grade may be only 30 percent. But without earning that 30 percent, it is impossible to obtain an A, a B, and probably even a C.

Homework is critical, but it does not have to take much time. Parkinson's Law states that *a task will expand to fit the time allotted to it.*[v] The study habits of most underperforming students show just how true that is. The goal of active studying is to use study time efficiently and limit the time spent studying. It will be time well spent.

As with active reading, active study sessions have distinct stages. The first stage is to set up and scope out the work, the second stage is to do the work, and the third stage is to pack up. Use active studying techniques in every study session.

SET UP AND SCOPE OUT THE WORK

Effective study spaces promote efficient work habits. It takes some thought and revision to develop an optimal study space.

Arrive at your study session ready to work. Eat something light before studying to shore up energy but not so much as to induce fatigue. Sit apart from other people who might disturb your concentration.

Some find that recall improves if music is playing softly in the background. Others find that this only works at the start of the study sessions. Once engaged, any sounds can be counterproductive and can intrude on concentration, such that even soft music can become distracting. Those who use music to help them settle in should turn it off if it becomes a distraction.

Study sessions start by taking an inventory of the work to be done. Make a list of subjects, organized into a task list, and establish a target time to complete each task. Set a "study completion time" for the overall session. This uses Parkinson's Law to advantage by limiting the time to complete the job, and it shines a light at the end of the tunnel that can provide a psychological boost. It can also promote an aggressive attitude to compete against the deadline, which can be helpful.

Today's assignments should not be the only thing on the task list. Review the calendar to see if there are any long-term assignments that should be built into the study session. Use a scratch pad, Microsoft Word, or an Excel spreadsheet to make a list of what needs to be done and how much time each task is likely to take. Do not confuse this "to-do" list with the weekly calendar; they are two very different things. This list deals only with today's short-term tasks and provides a roadmap for the current session.

Be sure to build time into the schedule to read ahead in each subject. The time allotted to read ahead should be about one-third of the overall time allotted, usually five to ten minutes. The best time to read ahead is just after completing the work while the information is still fresh in your mind.

After creating the task list, add a five- to ten-minute block at the end to organize for tomorrow. Finally, calculate the total minutes to *determine the time when you expect to complete the list.*

That time becomes the session goal. Write it down on the list and choose a reward to enjoy if you achieve the target time. Dinner is always a good motivation, but the reward might also be an episode of a favorite TV show, a run, or time with a friend. The reward provides an incentive to stay focused.

The next step in the setup process is to create a sequence for the tasks. Each student develops his or her own strategy for doing this. Some prefer to put the items that require the most intellectual effort first, so they can tackle these while energy is at its best. Another common approach is to work on the short, easy items first in order to quickly shorten the list.

Organizing the study session should take about five to ten minutes. This time is well spent. Once the list is made, the work is defined and you have a realistic idea of how long it will take. This can be very important psychologically. The list also helps to pace the work and prevents wasting time. Organization is the key to an efficient study session!

Here is a sample senior high school level study session schedule for a moderately heavy homework day. (Schedules for different levels should vary in content and length, but the approach will be similar.) Notice the session is designed to undertake the intense, problem- solving subjects first (math and chemistry) and puts the easier ones near the end. Notice also that there is time built in for a ten-minute break.

Breaks are especially important in longer study sessions because they ensure we maintain a clear and refreshed mind throughout. The break may take the form of a quick walk, a trip to the refrigerator, or a ten-minute power nap. Better yet, if at all possible go outside during the break. The change in lighting, fresh air, and motion all restore energy.

Subject	Assignment / Task	Estimated Time	Actual Time
Start Time		4:15 PM	
Math	Chapter 12 - Odd Problems	20	
	Read Ahead - Chapter 13	10	
Chemistry	Read Chapter 8 / Section 2 - Redux Equations	10	
	Problems 1 - 6	15	
	Read Ahead / Next Section - Chapter 8	10	
English	Read - *Hamlet* Act II	20	
	Create List of Characters	5	
	Read Ahead - Act III	10	
BREAK		10	
AP American History	Work on Outline for Civil War Term Paper (Long-Term Assignment)	15	
	Read Ahead - Chapter 17	10	
	Review - Dates from Last Chapter Notes	5	
Spanish	No Assignment	0	
	Review - Vocab	5	
	Read Ahead - Imperfect Tense	10	
Pack Up		10	
Total Time		2 Hours 45 Minutes	
Target End Time		7:00 PM	

The start time for this study session is 4:15 PM and it should take two hours and forty-five minutes to complete, so the target end time is 7:00 PM. Dinner is at seven-thirty, so it won't be necessary to work after dinner. Most people like to relax after dinner, so this will work out well.

NOW DO THE WORK

The next step is to execute the plan that was just made. Keep an eye on the clock and don't hesitate to modify the schedule as needed, either to delve into an unexpectedly difficult concept or to shorten the list if one of the tasks takes less time than originally anticipated. However, if a real roadblock emerges—such as a math problem that just doesn't make sense—put it aside and move on. Make a note to come back to it later after everything else is done. Do not allow one item to throw off the entire schedule.

Note the "actual" time you begin and end each task next to your estimates, especially during your first few study sessions, using a list. This will make it possible to create more accurate estimates in the future.

Write down any ideas or questions that need further study as they occur. This is particularly important when reading ahead to the next lesson. Take these notes to class and refer to them at the appropriate time.

Similarly, we often have important, useful ideas as we learn. Don't allow these thoughts to divert the process at hand but do jot them down for future reference. Also, note ideas related to other projects or things to remember to bring to class as you think of them.

Many assignments include an "Easter egg" left by the teacher for the alert student to find. These are generally some tasks or references they expect to follow up on later that can only be discovered by paying attention to detail. Write these down as you discover them and don't forget to act on them. Stay organized!

TIME TO PACK IT UP

The study session doesn't end until the work is packed up for the next day. Check the calendar again at this stage to avoid forgetting to prepare for any activities.

Packing sets the stage for the next day. Organize your backpack to make things easy to find:

- Set up folders and books by topic in order to have what you need when you need it.
- Keep related books, notes, assignments, and other materials together.

- Place assignments to be handed in on top, so it will be *impossible to ever forget* to turn in something that was completed.
- Always check the printer for forgotten items.

Packing up may also involve organizing a gym bag for practice or calling a friend to confirm afterschool plans.

After packing up, put everything in a place that makes it *impossible* to leave things behind. For example, put your backpack by the door and put your coat with it. Use the same place every day and develop a habit of checking that spot each time you leave the house. Another useful trick is to put the car keys with your books and bags so you cannot possibly leave them behind.

Develop a routine so that being organized becomes the new "normal." It will save a great deal of time and makes it easy to stay ahead.

Chapter 9: Key Points

- Active study sessions make study sessions efficient and limit the time spent studying.
- There are three stages:
  1. Set up and scope out the work.
     - Organized study space / good energy / avoid distractions
     - Review all the work to be done before starting.
     - Make a task list and assign times to each task.
     - Establish a completion date for the entire session.
  2. Do the work.
     - Stay on time and keep notes of items to follow up.
     - Do not become bogged down with problems—return to them later if needed.
  3. Pack it up.
     - Go through the schedule for the next day and organize accordingly.
     - Be sure not to leave anything behind—check the printer.
     - Put things where it will be impossible to forget them.
- Make being organized your new routine. It will save time.

Part 4

Making It Happen

> *"Are you bored with life? Then throw yourself into some work you believe in with all you heart, live for it, die for it, and you will find happiness that you had thought could never be yours."*
> —Dale Carnegie

CHAPTER 10
BE AN ACTIVE STUDENT

It should be clear that Active Learning is a skill. It is not an inborn talent. Skills take time and effort to develop. The more time spent practicing, the better the results. It may not be possible to master everything at once—that's OK. Active Learning skills improve over time. The most important step is to commit to using them—which is to say, take it seriously.

Few students are able to incorporate all the Active Learning techniques immediately. A good way to start is to practice one or two of each of the techniques at a time. Some are easier than others to master, such as organizing your work space and sitting "where the action is" in class. Others may take more time, such as active reading and active listening. The key to success is to keep the techniques in mind so as to make steady progress.

Refer back to this book periodically. A good time to do this is between semesters, after the grades are in. Evaluate your performance honestly, especially if the grades do not match your expectations. Were Active Learning techniques really used? Is there room for improvement?

> ### Skill Development Tip
>
> *The information in this book can take on added significance as you develop your Active Learning skills. Reviewing the concepts from time to time can be very helpful, particularly between semesters or at the start of a new year. Try explaining Active Learning techniques to friends who may need help. When you do, you may be impressed to realize how much you have improved!*

Over time, Active Learning becomes a lifestyle. Achievement becomes an attitude. Active learners don't approach courses as simple classes; they approach them as challenges. For active learners, performing well in a course presents a competition against others *and* themselves.

Be an Active Student

Having a realistic perspective about education can be motivating. Remember that school is not just about learning, grades, sports, or friends—it is about opportunity. It is about opening doors for those who achieve, and closing doors to those who do not. Whether you are rich or poor, go to a public school or private prep school, Active Learning techniques will improve your academic performance. These strategies are not difficult. Many are frankly common sense. Show up. Pay attention. Write things down. Be organized.

Unlike life as an adult, students in school have all the rules explained to them before they play the game. They know exactly what is expected, when it is due, and what to do to pass every assignment. Active learners take advantage of this. They pay attention to the instructions and aggressively carry them out.

The popular notion that the rich get richer while the poor get poorer applies very well to education. Some students are fortunate enough to come from families where the skills for success are taught from an early age. For most, these skills must be acquired elsewhere (such as by reading this book). Society opens doors to good students and locks underperforming students out. Those who are excluded may never even know what is inside. Do not let society lock out opportunities for you.

GOING BROADER: FOLLOW YOUR DREAMS

The great thing about having knowledge is that it can take us in many different directions. Not all doctors practice medicine. Many conduct research or work in administration. Not all lawyers practice law. Many run businesses, write books, or work in public policy. Not all geologists work in oil fields and not all marine biologists work in aquariums. They may help in construction, run aquaculture farms, or advise the fishing industry.

Knowledge leads to opportunities. There are a vast number of pathways life can follow. To gain a broad exposure to the possibilities, consider taking classes about new fields that may be completely unfamiliar. Explore business, music, or astrophysics. Even if you do not make them your career, the information will enrich your life and increase your knowledge of what is available.

It isn't necessary to have your life planned out in high school, but even those who are uncertain where their paths will lead them usually know what they enjoy doing and have some idea of what interests them. Allow yourself to dream. Imagine what your life will be like in ten, twenty, and thirty years. Pursue your interests, both in school and independently. Doing so can lead to unexpected rewards and open doors to opportunities that may be very satisfying.

Life goals are often governed by personal values. Some might want a job that provides a regular schedule, so there is time to come home in the early evenings to be with the family. Others may be moved to serve humanity, invent new technologies, or work to preserve the environment. Some consider money and income to be the priority. Whatever your interests are, look for opportunities to explore them.

For those interested in the top-earning occupations—which are often the jobs that require the most education—check out the table below:[vi] if you see a job that looks interesting, look it up on the Web. Find out the requirements and consider whether your current performance at school will support your goals. Anticipating where life may take you can affect how you approach learning.

Occupation	Hourly Wage (Average)	Annual Income (Average)
Surgeons	$105.66	$219,770
Anesthesiologists	$101.80	$211,750
Oral and Maxillofacial Surgeons	$101.30	$210,710
Orthodontists	$99.13	$206,190
Obstetricians/Gynecologists	$98.31	$204,470
Internists (General)	$88.46	$183,990
Family and General Practitioners	$81.03	$168,550
Chief Executives	$80.43	$167,280
Psychiatrists	$78.68	$163,660
Pediatricians (General)	$77.60	$161,410
Dentists (General)	$75.41	$156,850
Dentists (Specialists)	$73.83	$153,570
Podiatrists	$63.33	$131,730
Lawyers	$62.03	$129,020
Natural Sciences Managers	$61.06	$127,000
Prosthodontists	$60.29	$125,400
Engineering Managers	$59.04	$122,810
Computer/Info System Managers	$58.00	$120,640
Marketing Managers	$57.73	$120,070
Petroleum Engineers	$57.67	$119,960
Airline Pilots/Copilots/Engineers	Not Provided	$117,060

Note that the above data, from the American Bureau of Labor Statistics (BLS), does not include self-employed workers, entertainers, celebrities, or athletes, whose incomes might be much higher than those listed. For more detailed information on a broader scope of occupations and their wages, visit the BLS website (www.BLS.gov). It does not include the entire list of professions that exist but it does list the most popular jobs and their average salaries.

GRADES = MONEY

Good academic performance—and good grades—create opportunities. The opportunities may present in many forms—college admissions, scholarships, jobs, promotions, and relationships—but in the end, good grades translate into the ability to earn a better living, live a better life, and have more money.

Grades determine how high we are able to climb the "educational ladder." Where we step off significantly impacts the level at which we go through life.

Step off that ladder at the level *you* choose.

Maximize your performance and turn your grades into opportunities—and money—using the Active Learning techniques you learned in this book. Take school seriously. Start now. You will be glad you did.

> CHAPTER 10: KEY POINTS
>
> - Develop your Active Learning skills over time. Don't expect to become a star student overnight.
> - Refer back to this book from time to time. As your skills develop, different sections will take on different meanings.
> - Allow yourself to dream. Research potential jobs and evaluate whether your current approach to school will allow you to make your dreams a reality.
> - Act now! The effort will be worthwhile and the benefits will last a lifetime.

For more information, updates, and useful learning tools, visit www.GradesEqualMoney.com.

ENDNOTES

i   For an excellent reference on dyslexia, see *Essentials of Dyslexia Assessment and Intervention (Essentials of Psychological Assessment)* by Nancy Mather and Barbara J. Wendling (John Wiley and Sons, Hoboken, NJ 2011).

ii   Borg, John. *Body Language: 7 Easy Lessons to Master the Silent Language.* Prentice Hall Life, 2008

iii Paul Ekman, PhD. *Emotions Revealed, Second Edition: Recognizing Faces and Feelings to Improve Communication and Emotional Life.* Holt Paperbacks; 2nd edition, 2007

iv   Much has been written about memory techniques. The methods presented here apply well to the classroom. Other approaches can be helpful in other situations. Most methods rely on creating visual and auditory associations to bolster recall of information, and some can be quite elaborate. An excellent and entertaining review of memory techniques can be found in a book called *Moonwalking with Einstein* by Joshua Foer (Penguin Press, 2011).

v   C. Northcote Parkinson first proposed this concept in a book entitled *Parkinson's Law* in 1957. This delightful book is not only very entertaining, but it helps to train business executives around the world. I highly recommend this book for any student who wants to obtain better insight into human nature.

vi   For more information about wages for various professions, visit the Bureau of Labor and Statistics Web site at http://www.bls.gov/oes/2009/may/oes_nat.htm#(4).

AN AFTERWORD TO EDUCATORS

Most educational systems expect students to know how to learn. Learning is a skill, not a talent, and skills must be developed. This book uses a step-by-step approach to help students acquire learning skills.

The skills described in this book helped me do well in medical school. I wish I had known about them earlier. High school and college would have been much less stressful, and I would have performed better at every stage.

This book does not attempt to undermine the efforts of sophisticated educators or rewrite their philosophies on how to teach and learn. I write as a lifelong student, and I am directing my message at fellow students. Educators create the system. The Active Learning method provides students with tools to navigate the system.

The educational literature is replete with buzzwords. This makes it nearly impossible to write about learning without using words and phrases that may be interpreted differently by different people. This book may use terms that may not conform to their formal definitions. The concept of "Active Learning," for example, has different meanings for different authors, as do the terms "active listening" and "active reading." If so, this is not intentional, and I apologize to anyone who may be offended if my use does not agree with theirs.

This book isn't directed at educators but rather at students. For the record, the Active Learning System described in this book is my own. Nobody taught it to me and, to my knowledge, it isn't available anywhere else. Of course, much of this system is based on common sense, and many others have tried to do what I'm trying to do here—help students to learn—which is terrific. Any overlap in my terminology, methods, or ideas with any other system is purely coincidental.

Nothing in this book encourages cheating. Unfortunately, there are no shortcuts to learning, unless you consider the advice to "do it right the first time, so you don't have to do it again" to be a shortcut. While I don't consider high number or letter grades to be the primary goal of learning, I do recognize that grades are the currency that purchases opportunities. The emphasis here is on improving learning but make no mistake about it—a major goal of this book is to help students improve their grades so they can earn a better living as adults.

An Afterword to Educators

I spend a significant amount of time with young people and am often asked to speak with underperforming students to try to motivate them to do better. Over time, the foundations of these conversations have shaped what I now call the "Active Learning System." In many cases, the results of my conversations with underperforming students have led to dramatic improvements in their performances at school.

I believe this information should be available to everyone, so I've written this book. People spend huge amounts of money on tutors to help students learn what they should have learned at school. This book may help reduce that need.

Speaking to young people is different than writing a book. Books cannot respond to facial expressions. Books cannot take on a sympathetic tone when a student needs reassurance or a challenging tone when he or she isn't responding. But books can be far more available than I can be. They are also more patient and more consistent.

I hope you find this book useful.

Guy M. Kezirian, MD, FACS

ACKNOWLEDGMENTS

Many people have contributed to this book and without them it would not have been written. I am very grateful to all.

Foremost I would like to thank the students who read the various drafts of the manuscript for their frank and helpful comments, particularly Alexis, Olivia, Anthony, Evan, Colby, and Nicole; my wife, Mary, for tolerating my need to revise and revise again and for her unwavering support throughout this quixotic project; Arnold Heflin, the accomplished author of the inspiring novel *Mockingbird's Song*, for his gentle suggestions to keep at it and for pointing out the light at the end of the tunnel even when it was far off; Lindsey Patterson, whose expertise in adolescent development added great insights, and whose wonderful skill with words smoothed many rough edges off this work.

I would also like to thank the many teachers who challenged me to learn and made it necessary to develop the system described in this book. Their great passion and high standards made me a better student. I hope their influence is conveyed to the students who read this book.

ABOUT THE AUTHOR

Guy Kezirian is a life-long learner who lives in Scottsdale, Arizona. He is a board-certified ophthalmologist who is active in clinical research and consulting through his company, SurgiVision® Consultants, Inc.

Dr. Kezirian attended McGill University in Montreal, Quebec, Canada, where he obtained a Bachelor of Science in neurosciences. He obtained his medical degree from Brown University in Providence, Rhode Island, and completed his clinical training at the Faulkner Hospital near Boston, at Lennox Hill Hospital in New York City, and at Albany Medical College.

He is the father of four grown children. He served in several volunteer positions with the Boy Scouts of America for more than a decade and as a Grand Awards judge and Section Chair at the Intel International Science and Engineering Fair since 2005. His current projects include an analysis of best practices in medical research and a separate venture to expand healthcare options in the field of consumer-based Lifestyle medicine.

For more information, updates, and useful learning tools, visit www.GradesEqualMoney.com

Printed in Germany
by Amazon Distribution
GmbH, Leipzig